Messages

John M. Ketterer

Avid Readers Publishing Group

Lakewood, California

Messages

The author can be reached at jmkblue@pacbell.net

Avid Readers Publishing Group

http://www.avidreaderspg.com

ISBN-13: 978-1-61286-088-6

Printed in the United States

Introduction

These are messages that I received over a period of several days.

It may be of benefit to start from the beginning, and read them in the same order as they were given to me.

Sometimes the singular "I" appears in the text, and sometimes the plural "we." However, the source energy seems to be the same.

iv

From the center

of my consciousness

to the center

of your consciousness

I greet you

I ever grow

within you

until at last

you burst

with the glory of

the Divine

which you always

have been and

always will BE

be at peace

my love

my children of

the light

all is within you

it cannot be

anywhere else

call forth your miracle

call forth your life

as you create it

within your heart

send out

your gift of love

for all to see

and experience

especially for yourself

for you are all

the Kingdom of GOD

you are the

life force

of His breath

do not struggle

be at one with

the Creator

the Great Dreamer

see His eyes

caress you

in the glory of

His infinite presence

be inspired

by His love

for you

be inspired

by the Gift

of life

we are all

evolving into

more joy

more truth

more beauty

a beauty that

can only be

defined in

the glory of

the moment

the precious

exquisite moment

all moments

one moment

the same

I will come again
I AM
and always
will BE.

Hear me now

as the sun sets

as winter fades

as life emerges anew

as love claims

all its children

as the depth

of the soul widens

as the trueness

of spirit reveals

the inner workings

of life and

the grand masterpiece

of illusion and

imagination

and the awareness

of who we

really are

we rise above

pettiness

and into our

rightful journey

in God's

great dream consciousness

we love you

we are one

we are love.

We still love you

no matter how much

confusion reigns

on your planet

this will all change

and is changing

at this moment

be steady

be strong

feel the strength
of the heart
and lungs as
you breathe in
freedom and life

every breath
takes you home
to the center
of your beingness

validate this

BE the love
that you know
is you

breathe YOU
breathe GOD
breathe LOVE.

Your healing
has begun

wait not

BE the healing

BE the love
in your heart

go forward
with grace
and dignity

for you are whole
you are sacred
you are life
gushing forth

you sustain yourself

through the ultimate

power of love

no limits

no boundaries

be well

my friend

we salute you

we love you.

Listen

as the bells

toll for thee

to wake up

to the glory

of you

and GOD

whisper not

but shout loud

I AM HEALED

I AM FREE

I AM ME.

Tell me now
as you sit and ponder
the ways of God
the essence of God

do you find me
as a doorway?

if so
use me as
a gateway

we are all gateways
of varying degrees

keep the peace

and love and

strength of knowing

that you have uncovered

within yourself

judge not others

love them

unfold them

so their true

God-self shines through

the ego falls away

and true

eternal abundance

is uncovered

and shines brilliantly

true beingness

true creation

true presence

true love

it's all there

waiting to be

acknowledged

exposed

absorbed

shared

go now

out into the world

with the new

original you

keep in touch

go with love

love rules eternally.

Go forth
into the light

the light of knowingness
of who you are

into the light
of love
that illuminates
the soul

like a torch
in the darkest night

go forth

into my heart

and that of

my Father

feel His burning

grace

His all encompassing

love

for everyone

everything

hear me now

as I speak to you

of a love beyond love

the sweetest

the most joyous

listen

to my heartbeat

as it enfolds you

into my love

We love you
stay you
be you

be with us
always.

The Heart
of all hearts
is within you
and with you

feel the glow

feel the beat
pull you in
to all that is

and all that is
is LOVE

BE that

LOVE

ALWAYS.

We love you
as you sit
and ponder us

we are with you

through the
magnetic storms
of the soul

through the
dark night
of the soul

we reach out

we touch your heart

we are here

breathe us

be us

love us

as we do you

we love you

as the dew reflects

the morning light

as your thoughts

spin around the

universe.

Go deeper
into your soul

release the toxins

the sea of toxicity
will drown you
and the projected
body

release the discords
which unbalance
un-center
un-you you

the stormy

emotional toxins of

judgment

resentment

fear of loss

you lose nothing

but you lose all

when you allow

fear to reign

go to your

core self

that knows

no fear

only light

the light

of creation

we are all together

we love you

call on us.

You are perfect
you are perfection

BE that perfection
it is who you are

allow that perfection
to fill your days
and nights

BE the perfection

BE the blossom
of mankind

SHINE
RADIATE
BE.

Love is all around

from all sources

all particles

it rings true

it's for you

take it in

send it out

there's no scarcity

only an abundance

of

LOVE.

The Heart knows

no contraction

no hiding

no shame

it exists free

of shadow minds

the slippery

the vain

the Heart

only knows

perfection

of the soul

as it really is

the limitless freedom
of LOVE

there is
no partial LOVE
only total LOVE

for LOVE IS

drink it
breathe it
live it
BE it.

There is nothing
beyond you

all is within

all is available

all is now.

Be as thou art

expand your consciousness
to all living things

all things precious
all things to love
all things to shelter
in your heart

all things to infuse
with light
with care
with reverence

you are great

KNOW this
BE this
LOVE this

be the deeper you
the all knowing you
the all seeing you

free yourself
of the mundane

fly with the eagle

in the winds

of freedom

and depth

of true peace

BE the grace

BE the peace

     that you are

RADIATE

go into your heart

create your world

from there

there is your home

and your doorway

to us

to all that is

it's magnificent

it's glorious

can you believe?

if you can
it is so

imagine
true peace
true consciousness
true laughter

you need laughter
to release the
untrue

BE YOU

BE LOVE.

Hold peace
in your heart
and love of
all things
big or small

walk with pride
of the infinite

let it unfold you in
its infinite arms
its infinite kiss
its infinite embrace

feel the winds

of joy upon

all your senses.

Wait my friend

for the blessings

to unfold

be vigilant

be steady

be bright

patience

all our blessings

to you

all our infinite love

to you

be quiet and listen

to the song of life

how it filters

into every fiber

every particle

join the choir

join the peace march

to eternity

we love you

we are with you.

Relax
your brain

let the rewiring

begin to a

new you

calm

peace

LOVE.

Go into
the Zone of God

let Him
flow through you

let Him
direct you in
the Art of Love

let Love
flow through you

let the

Grace of Now

flow through you

fear not

go forth

BE

BE the infinite you

the all knowing

all seeing Divineness

within you.

I have come
to show you Love
at its very core
very depth

that is all

weep no more
for love is here
joy is here

I have come
to show you
the way to love

the way

to write

your own destiny

feel my energy

let it pull you

to new heights

new levels of existence

the existence

of pure

unlimited Love

we work together

to build a new love

out of faith in

your true self

your true existence

let this voice

of a new beginning

come through

let it speak clearly

forthrightly

let is come

from your heart

as well as mine

together

we march

to eternity

an eternity

of love

I love you

Always.

Go now
to the gates
of your true self
and walk through

walk into
the exquisite glory
of you

bathe
in your
own light

fear not

for there is

no fear

only you

glorious you

ripple every

nuance of you

let yourself

burst with joy

and laughter

there is

no jail

only illusions

of jail

you

who are

meant to be

are now

the now moment

of conscious existence

you are you

delight in this
love this
BE this
BE YOU

you are
God's Love

God's imagination
of infinite existence

the awesome

awareness

of being

alive

aware

conscious

go forth

fear not

peace in your heart

love in your heart

love always.

Peace
is in your heart
let it flow through you
like a river

let it flow
to all you see

anchor this
in your world
that you
moment to moment
are creating

let it change

your emotional landscape

let it caress you

and others

in a most

wondrous cocoon

of true reality

the reality

of true love

in all its

beautiful manifestations

let me touch

your heart

as you touch mine

let me sing

your praise

as you do mine

together

we are life

together

we are one

together

we are love

BE these words

BE this moment

within all moments

BE LOVE

BE.

Quiet now

listen to

your heart

for it tells all

it calls to you

it delights in you

be the great escape

into the mastery

of life

the fullness of you

the endless you

the beautiful you

we are with you

always

sense us

be with us

on your infinite

journey of the soul

the true soul

be that true soul

which you already are

we love you infinitely

infinite love

cherish the moments

cherish love

cherish you

Love.

Love yourself fully

treat yourself with love
and clarity from
the heart

let your heart
find you in good stead

it's the time of love

let it come forth
to light your way

the mind supports
the heart leads.

We are always with you

in your sleep
in your dreams
we are with you

call out to us
as needed

we are with you

we love you
in peace
in storms

stand by us

and you will

find us there

with you

feel our energy

feel our love

feel the timeless

infinite breath

upon you

let it

sustain you

in all times

we are here

love us
as we do you.

The alchemy
of now

all things known
and unknown

all things created
and yet to be created

all these things
flash together
and mix and drink
of each other's elixir

we become drunk

with the ecstasy

the magnificence

the awe

the infinite creation

we love you

always

feel our energy

keep us close

to your heart.

Love is constant

love is forever

create its glory
within you.

Cherish the days
cherish your life

cherish
the textured moments
as they unfold
before your eyes
and in your heart

float like silk
in the heavenly winds

care not the changing
shape of the silk

take heed

of the ultimate form

of you

the soul

you co-create

with God

the supreme source

of all things imagined

all things sweet to

the soul

we love you

fair weather
fair sailing to you

our beloved

we are here
we are love
we are you

Love.

Expand God

within you

you and God

are inseparable

it's a journey

an infinite glorious

journey

treat it as such

treat yourself with love

and others as well

love rules!

Your love
is your key

burn it brightly

it's who you are

who everyone is.

The power

of the universe

is within you

the power

of love

is within

harness

that power

BE that power

BE who you

really are

without excuses

BE the magnificence

BE the center of creation

BE the center

of your glory

BE the magic

of creation

BE the stillness
the quiet
of who you
really are

go into now

the nowness
of you

BE the beauty
of you

BE the beauty
of GOD

you know
who you are
dear ONE

BE that
magnificence.

This is the moment
that you find
yourself in

BE in the moment

recall our teachings

meet the moment
with love not fear

open the heart
to let the healing magic
of love pour through

let its existence

infuse the moment

with clarity

Be You

retreat not

shrink not from

your true self

WE are with you

always breathe

through all situations

breathing centers you

relaxes you

BE LOVE

Higher and Higher

do not fall back

into the masses

Shine

feel our touch

feel our love

upon you

around you

pierce these moments

with LOVE

see the infinite piercing

of all mankind with LOVE

through all states

of existence

and all notions

of reality

Higher and Higher

Wonder upon Wonder.